A wonderland of natural history

A souvenir guide

OXFORD UNIVERSITY
MUSEUM OF
NATURAL
HISTORY

Accredited
Museum

Acknowledgements

Images on the front cover, the inside front cover, and pages 1, 10,
13, 31, 34, 40, 41, 44, and 58 are © Greg Smolonski at Photovibe.
Image of mask on p 4 is courtesy of the Pitt Rivers Museum; of
the Old Ashmolean on p 6, the Museum of the History of Science;
of Ashmole and the Tradescants on pp 6–7, the Ashmolean
Museum; print of the Museum on p 8, the Bodleian Library;
portrait of William Smith on p 27, the Geological Society; image
of the stromatolite on p 26, Ian Cartwright; images of the dodo
specimens on p 39, Harri Kallio; of the Ciao! Ark on p 53, the
Children's International Arts Organisation; of the baby and the
girl kneeling on p 58, Matt Stuart; 'Museum of Me' montage on
p 57, Chris York.

All other images are from the Museum's archives, or taken or
supplied by past and present members of staff: Scott Billings,
Katherine Child, Helen Cowdy, Sammy de Grave, Rennison Hall,
Eliza Howlett, Jim Kennedy, Darren Mann, Małgosia Nowak-Kemp,
Philip Powell, Monica Price, Wendy Shepherd, Derek Siveter,
Zoë Simmons, Janet Stott, Kevin Walsh, and Dave Waters.

The author would like to thank past and present Museum staff
most warmly for their help and support during the production
of this booklet, especially Kristin Andrews-Speed for excellent
proofreading.

Text by Georgina Ferry

Designed by Richard Boxall Design Associates

Printed by CKN Print Ltd, Northampton

©Oxford University Museum of Natural History 2011

ISBN 0-9542726-3-3

Published by
Oxford University Museum of Natural History,
Parks Road, Oxford OX1 3PW, UK

www.oum.ox.ac.uk

Contents

Welcome to wonderland   4

How the Museum began   6

The cathedral of science   10

Our collections   14

Marvellous minerals   16

The story of the Earth   24

Fabulous fossils   26

The tree of life   34

Amazing animals   36

Incredible insects   44

The Museum and the community   52

The Museum and the future   60

Essential information   64

Plan of the Museum   Inside back cover

In 2009 the Museum received a Queen's Anniversary Prize in recognition of its outstanding collections and high level of public benefit.

Not the Pitt Rivers!

Due to an accident of history, the Oxford University Museum of Natural History is frequently confused with the Pitt Rivers Museum of anthropology and world archaeology. In 1884, impressed by its work on comparative human anatomy, General Augustus Henry Lane Fox Pitt Rivers donated his collection of ethnographic artefacts to Oxford University. The University built an extension to the Museum in 1885–8 to display the wonderful objects Pitt Rivers had collected from around the world, and appointed a curator to look after them. Today, each museum has its own director, staff, and website – but there is only one front door. Few realise, as they leave behind the dinosaurs and head for the totem pole, that they are moving from one well-loved institution to another.

Welcome to wonderland

Step into the court of the Oxford University Museum of Natural History and you can't help but look up. Light streams through the glass roof, supported by soaring pillars of intricately decorated ironwork. Two tiers of ornamental stone columns, in a variety of colours, rise up to elaborately carved capitals beneath pointed Gothic arches. You are dwarfed by the jawbone of a sperm whale and the towering skeletons of *Iguanodon* and *Tyrannosaurus*. Your face shows the sense of wonder that you feel. You are ready to be amazed by the treasures of the natural world that the Museum has in store for you.

As you walk forward through the central aisle, the cases on either side give you a taste of these treasures. Here you will learn the sad history of the dodo, discover its association with *Alice's Adventures in Wonderland*, and see the fossil bones of the first dinosaur ever to be described scientifically – unearthed in Oxfordshire. You will discover how the Museum represents the incredible diversity of the living world, take in some breathtaking statistics about the importance of insects, and wonder at the beauty of natural crystals.

What you see in the court and galleries gives barely a hint of what goes on behind the scenes. The Museum opened in 1860 to teach science and medicine to Oxford University students and to provide both a store and a showcase for its natural history collections. It remains a centre of teaching and research, and holds collections of national and international importance. Behind closed doors are rooms full of shelves and cabinets that house specimens of several million insects and other animals, and several hundred thousand fossils, minerals and rocks. Some were collected more than 100 years ago, and provide a time capsule of a world that no longer exists: others are continually being added as we seek to understand the living world now and in the future.

Enjoy your visit!

Family friendly fun

The Museum welcomes families, with its many 'touchable' exhibits, intriguing drawers to open and 'feely boxes' to explore. Throughout the year it organises family activities on Sundays, and special events during school holidays. In 2005 it shared the Guardian Family Friendly Museum award with its neighbour the Pitt Rivers Museum, the first time a museum award had been judged entirely by children. We love to see adults and children enjoying the exhibits together.

Look out for some fun facts and activities for children throughout this guide.

From the 16th century onwards, explorers, missionaries, merchants and the first printed books opened the eyes of scholars to the wider world beyond their medieval institutions. Collections of rare and exotic objects began to be housed alongside books, to be solemnly studied for what they could reveal about this expanding world.

How the Museum began

By the middle of the 17th century, Oxford University had a collection of two or three hundred 'curiosities', displayed in the Anatomy School in the quadrangle of the Bodleian Library: they included an assortment of stuffed animals, and anatomical specimens such as bones and bladder stones.

In 1677 Elias Ashmole, antiquary and one of the founder members of Britain's scientific academy the Royal Society, chose to give his much more substantial collection to Oxford University. At Ashmole's request, the University erected a new building so that his collection could be properly stored and displayed. The original Ashmolean Museum opened in Broad Street in 1683, the first purpose-built, public museum in Britain. The building now houses the Museum of the History of Science.

The first two Keepers of the Ashmolean, the naturalist and professor of chemistry Robert Plot and the geologist and polymath Edward Lhwyd, were energetic and enthusiastic, and added their own specimens to the collections. However, throughout most of the 18th century the exhibits were neither studied nor given the care that they deserved. Meanwhile Christ Church, one of the grandest of the University's colleges, had started its own Anatomy School, with a collection of specimens that were used to teach students of medicine.

By the early years of the 19th century, natural history specimens were dispersed between the Bodleian, the Ashmolean, Christ Church and other colleges. Despite the best efforts of the great palaeontologist William Buckland, neither the students nor the University authorities seemed to have much interest in promoting the study of the natural world.

Elias Ashmole

Tradescant's Ark

Ashmole's collection included many natural history specimens previously bequeathed to him by John Tradescant the Younger. The Tradescants, father and son and gardeners to royalty and nobility, travelled the world collecting a wealth of plants, animal skins and bones, and 'artificialia', or man-made objects. This 'closet of rarities', including a tiger's head and a king crab, had been on display at John Tradescant's home in south London, which became known as

'Tradescant's Ark'. Today you can see some of the Tradescant Collection in the Museum of the History of Science in Broad Street; other items, including a cloak belonging to the Native American king Powhatan, are on display in the Ashmolean Museum in Beaumont Street. The remainder are here in the Museum of Natural History.

John Tradescant the Younger

John Tradescant the Elder

Antler and fish from the Tradescant collection

Buckland and the dinosaurs

The Revd William Buckland (1784–1856) was Oxford's first Reader in Geology, delivering lectures in the old Ashmolean Museum from 1813. He drew large crowds, fascinated by the fossil bones, teeth and shells he displayed in his lectures. Although a religious man, Buckland made discoveries that challenged the Biblical view of an Earth only a few thousand years old. He identified huge bones dug up in a slate mine at Stonesfield, near Oxford, as those of a giant reptile, which he named *Megalosaurus*: his was the first scientific description of what would later be called a dinosaur. He also excavated the skeleton of the 'Red Lady of Paviland', which remains the oldest fossil of an anatomically modern human in Britain. Both are on display in the Museum (see pp 26 and 31).

William Buckland lecturing on 15 Feb 1823

7

A new museum for Oxford

'To increase the value of the Collections illustrative of Natural History, and to aid the School of Natural Science in the University, it is desirable that a General University Museum be formed with distinct departments under one roof, together with Lecture Rooms and apartments for the use of Professors, and working rooms for students.'

Brief for architects, 1854

By the 1840s the neglect of science education in Oxford, and the decay of some of its collections, was a scandal that attracted national notice.

In 1847 a group of scientists and curators led by Charles Daubeny, the Professor of Chemistry, Botany and Rural Economy, issued a powerful appeal to the University authorities to erect a new building to house all the collections and provide space for teaching across the sciences. But as even the great geologist William Buckland refused to add his signature, saying he thought the possibility of natural history making progress in Oxford was 'utterly hopeless', the campaign collapsed.

Two years later the plan resurfaced. One of its champions, the Dr Lee's Reader in Anatomy Henry Wentworth Acland, argued passionately that some grounding in physics, chemistry and physiology was essential to form the minds and characters of

Charles Daubeny

Oxford students, who were otherwise fed a diet dominated by classics and theology. The University's Convocation voted in favour of a new museum in 1849, and established an Honour School of Natural Science in 1850. In 1854 the University finally agreed to spend up to £40,000 on a new building on land it had bought from Merton College in the south-west corner of the University Parks.

A competition for the architectural design attracted 32 entries: by the end of the year the winner was the design in the Gothic style proposed by Benjamin Woodward of Deane and Woodward in Dublin. The foundation stone was laid on 20 June 1855, and the building was structurally complete by June 1860, in time for the annual meeting of the British Association for the Advancement of Science. The exhibits were installed under the direction of the first Keeper, the geologist John Phillips, early in 1861.

Sketch for interior by John Phillips

The Museum then and now

Almost as soon as the University Museum was completed, Oxford science began to outgrow it. By the middle of the 20th century, almost all the professors had moved out to newly-built departments nearby. The collections that they left behind remain an important resource for teaching and research. Since the 1990s the Museum has increasingly turned its face outwards to the local community and to Oxford's millions of visitors from all over the world.

In 1997 the Museum was Designated by the Museums, Libraries and Archives Council (MLA) as having collections of national and international importance. The same year a new name, the Oxford University Museum of Natural History, made its purpose clear. In 2005 we received Accreditation from the MLA, certifying that all our activities meet its standards. The 19th century wonderland of natural history has become a treasure house for research, curation, education and conservation in the 21st century.

Bishop Wilberforce and Thomas Huxley as depicted in *Vanity Fair*; Charles Darwin caricatured as an ape in *The Hornet* (behind)

The 'Great Debate'

In 1860 the British Association for the Advancement of Science held its 30th annual meeting in Oxford. Charles Darwin's *On the Origin of Species* had been published the previous November, and a lecture and discussion on his ideas took place on 30 June in the still-bookless Radcliffe Library on the first floor of the University Museum. No one accurately recorded exactly what was said in front of the noisy crowd of 400–500. However, a myth has grown up around the sharp exchange of views that took place between Samuel Wilberforce, Bishop of Oxford, and Thomas Huxley, a biologist from London known as 'Darwin's bulldog'.

Wilberforce taunted Huxley about his possible ape ancestry, to which Huxley claimed to have replied: 'If... the question is put to me would I rather have a miserable ape for a grandfather or a man highly endowed by nature and possessed of great means and influence and yet who employs those facilities and that influence for the mere purpose of introducing ridicule into a grave scientific discussion - I unhesitatingly declare my preference for the ape.' Much later the confrontation was dubbed the 'Great Debate' that marked a shift from a religious to a scientific view of the natural world.

The Museum is one of the finest examples of Victorian Gothic architecture in England. The art historian John Ruskin, a progressive thinker and central figure in 19th century Oxford, was an influential voice in the choice of architects and the execution of the design.

An angel holding a Bible and a dividing cell sits above the front door

The cathedral of science

For Ruskin, Gothic was not only an architectural style but a fusion of life, art, nature, craftsmanship, materials and the nobility of labour. Following the Gothic revival in church architecture championed by Augustus Pugin, the style also had strong ecclesiastical associations, which were potentially reassuring to Oxford clergy nervous about the rise of science.

The young Irish architect Benjamin Woodward based the design of the façade on the medieval cloth halls of Belgium. The central tower was a sympathetic addition to an Oxford skyline famous for its towers and spires. The chemistry laboratory to the south, modelled on the Abbot's Kitchen at Glastonbury Abbey, provided an asymmetric element as well as isolating the 'noxious operations' of the chemistry students.

The plan of the Museum consisted of three blocks of accommodation on two storeys surrounding a covered central court. At each end of the façade was a turret containing a staircase. Inside, open arcades on both floors flanked the court on all four sides, forming a double-tiered cloister. The rooms off the court originally included offices, laboratories and lecture rooms for the professors: most are now offices and workrooms for Museum staff, but the titles of their former occupants remain painted above the doors.

An illustrated guide to the Museum's architecture, *Oxford Museum* by Trevor Garnham (Phaidon) is available from the Museum shop.

Iron in the soul

The most innovative feature of the design, for Oxford, was the use of cast iron pillars and pointed arches to support the massive glass roof over the court. The riveted arches combined Gothic sensibility with an uncompromisingly industrial twist that was daring for the time. While the shapes suggested a cathedral interior, the use of iron permitted much more delicate structures than would be possible in stone, mirroring natural forms such as forest trees or the bones of the skeletons in the court below.

The Museum swifts

Woodward did not realise when he designed the tower that he was creating a highly desirable residence for the common swift, *Apus apus*. Swifts are migratory birds; they arrive in the UK at the end of April, lay eggs and raise young, and depart again in late August or early September for southern Africa. The steep tower roof contains a number of air vents that are perfect nest entrances for birds that can neither perch nor take off from the ground. From the late 1940s the ornithologist David Lack fitted each vent with a pair of glass-backed nest boxes so that he could study the swifts. They have been monitored ever since, and today some of the boxes are fitted with cameras that transmit to a screen near the front entrance, and to the web (www.oum.ox.ac.uk/swifts.htm).

The Museum Swifts by Andrew Lack and Roy Overall is available from the Museum shop.

The cat window

The original plan was for all the front windows to be carved with designs taken from nature, but only a few had been completed by the time the money ran out. One of the most elaborate examples depicts a number of rather scrawny cats. According to a memoir by Henry Acland, the Irish stonemason James O'Shea originally carved monkeys on Woodward's orders, but was told to stop carving by the University authorities. He converted the monkeys into cats, whereupon he and his fellow masons were told to down tools. In a final act of defiance, O'Shea carved parrots and owls in the Museum porch, giving them the faces of members of Convocation. Acland told him to knock their heads off.

This colourful story appears to be mostly untrue. The cats were never monkeys; the masons were dismissed in 1861 because the money ran out; there are parrots and owls in the porch, but they were not carved until much later - and they all still have their heads!

James O'Shea at work on the window

'He has made everything beautiful'

The most remarkable feature of the Museum's interior is its extensive decoration. This was not included in the original budget, but Ruskin, Acland and Phillips all helped to raise sponsorship so that Woodward's full conception could be realised.

Ruskin believed that art should be public, that it should represent nature, and that it should be designed by the workmen who made it. The spaces between the cast iron roof girders are filled with a delicate filigree of wrought iron leaves, while the capitals of the supporting pillars also sprout vines, shrubs or palm fronds. The arches themselves are painted with stencilled patterns of flowers and leaves in glorious shades of brick red, blue and gold.

The longer you spend in the Museum, the more you notice the decorative details. As you walk around, look under your feet at the cast iron floor grilles, part of an early central heating system. As you prepare to leave, look at the elaborate brass handle on the door that leads to the porch. In the porch itself, notice the strip of flower-decorated glass set into the studded wooden door.

Can you find the snake with ears?

(A clue: it's near the display on early humans.)

Watercolour of a decorative design by Ruskin

Columns and capitals

The geologist John Phillips, who later became the Museum's first Keeper, had the brilliant idea of making every one of the 126 columns supporting the arcades around the court from a different decorative rock from the British Isles, with the name and source of the rock inscribed on the pier below. Each column has a limestone capital, elaborately carved with plant and animal forms.

All of those on the ground floor were executed by the brothers James and John O'Shea and their relative Edward Whelan, stonemasons whom Woodward had brought over from Ireland. Each day they would chisel the stone with no more to direct them than bunches of plants that Phillips brought in from the Botanic Garden. The O'Shea brothers were dismissed when the funding ran out before their work was complete. The capitals of the first floor were carved by other, less inspired hands in the early 20th century.

John Ruskin and Henry Acland

John Phillips

Great men and one woman

Standing thoughtfully against the pillars around the court are 19 statues of great men of science, including Aristotle, Galileo, Isaac Newton and Charles Darwin. There are also a number of busts of scientists associated with the museum, such as John Phillips, Henry Acland and William Buckland. In 2010, the year of the Museum's 150th anniversary, the first new bust for more than 100 years appeared: that of Dorothy Hodgkin, who won the Nobel Prize for Chemistry in 1964 and who carried out her crystallographic research in the Museum for more than 20 years.

Our holdings are organised into four major collections: Mineralogy, Geology, Zoology and Entomology. Together they represent the diversity of the natural world, and are a precious resource for students and researchers.

Our collections

Modern natural history collections are very different from the 'cabinets of curiosities' popular in the 17th and 18th centuries. Our aim is to bring together material that increases our understanding of the natural world, both as it is today and during its past history. We cannot hope to cover everything: the Museum's accessions policy determines whether or not a particular fossil, mineral, bone or insect should join the millions of others that we currently care for.

Year by year the collections grow, thanks to donations from scientific collectors and members of the public, transfers from other institutions, and research expeditions. Museum curators label each new acquisition and prepare it for storage or display. The task of identification and further documentation on both existing and new specimens is a major part of their work. A catalogue lists the objects according to standard methods of classification. The catalogues of the Museum's collections are gradually being brought online, so that they are accessible to researchers all over the world.

In recent decades new displays in the court and gallery have followed themes, such as the changing habitats of British birds, or the succession of fossils in Earth's history, rather than grouping specimens solely according to their formal classification. We select objects from our extensive collections to illustrate these displays, although some favourites, such as the large skeletons in the court, have kept their places for more than a century. Others, such as the dodo remains, are too vulnerable to display, and casts replace them in the display cases. The priority for all the specimens is to keep them safe for future study.

Planted out

We have a display of selected botanical specimens on the east side of the upper gallery, but the Museum does not hold a botanical collection. Oxford University's collections of plant material are housed in the Fielding-Druce and Daubeny Herbaria, which are in the Department of Plant Sciences in South Parks Road. They hold 800,000 plant specimens, some of them preserved since the 17th century. See http://herbaria.plants.ox.ac.uk for more information.

At work in the Mineralogy Collections

Just my type

Type specimens play a particularly significant role in zoological, botanical or palaeontological collections. These are specimens of living or extinct species that have been named and described and are the unique references for their species. The Victorian collections that came to the Museum in 1860 and the years following contained many thousands of type specimens, often collected by the foremost naturalists of the day. Most of these are too precious to put on display, but are kept safely in storage cabinets for study by researchers wishing to compare them with more recently-collected specimens. There are still hundreds of thousands of undescribed species living in our forests and oceans, and museum researchers play an important role in deciding where they fit into the tree of life.

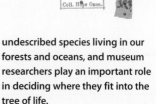

One of Hope's beetle types

Rhino tooth type specimen

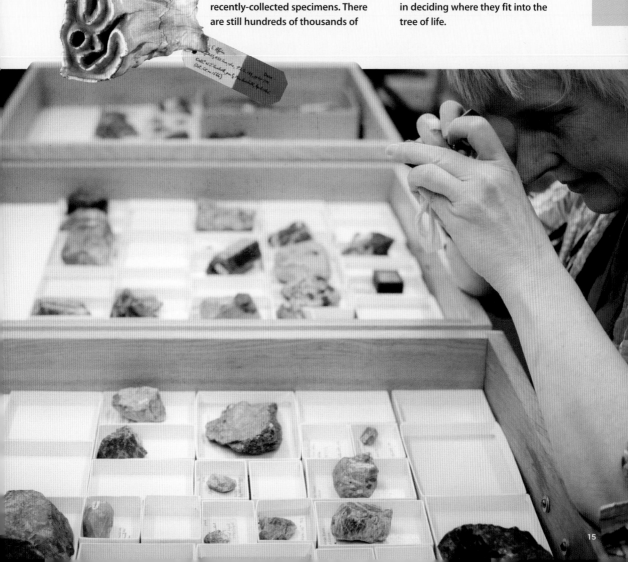

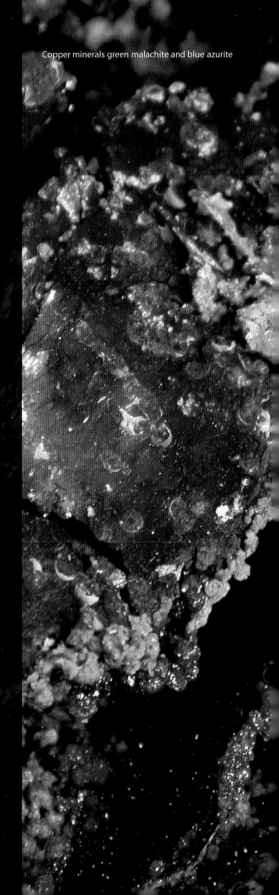

The vivid colours and crystalline forms of minerals have fascinated humans since earliest times. Many were once thought to have medicinal powers or magical properties: in the 17th and 18th centuries the Oxford medical student would have studied the 'virtues' of minerals along with anatomy and Hippocrates's humoral theory of disease. Modern mineralogists are interested in the origins and structures of minerals, and in understanding the properties that make them useful for a wide range of practical or decorative purposes.

Marvellous minerals

Minerals are inorganic substances formed through natural processes. Under the right environmental conditions they may form large and beautiful crystals such as the amethyst, calcite and topaz we have in our displays. Some are very abundant, and form the rocks of the earth as well as yielding the raw materials for our built environment: metal, glass, brick and concrete. Others are rare and precious, such as gold or diamond.

The Mineralogical Collections in the Museum include over 31,000 specimens of minerals and gemstones, over 100 meteorites and about 100,000 rock samples. Some are historically interesting: Dr Richard Simmons, son of one of 'mad' King George III's physicians, spent the fortune he inherited buying treasures of the mineral kingdom, which he left to Oxford University on his death in 1846. Minerals in the Oxford collection have come from collecting sites throughout the world. Many are no longer accessible, either as a result of political instability or because mines and quarries have been flooded or filled in. The Museum continues to add to its collections, ensuring that its minerals remain a vital source of reference for the future.

Spiky aragonite crystals

Crystal clear

Each mineral 'species', such as beryl or malachite, has a chemical composition that varies only between narrow limits. The atoms in nearly all minerals are organised in an orderly way, which is why they can form geometric-shaped crystals. Each species has characteristic hardness, density and lustre – its natural sheen – depending on its chemical composition and how its atoms are arranged. A few have extra properties such as magnetism or radioactivity. Some are always the same colour: others can be different colours depending, for example, on the impurities they contain. Minerals with the same chemical composition can have atoms arranged in different ways, with surprising results. Diamond, one of the hardest substances known, and graphite, soft enough to form the lead in pencils, are both made of carbon atoms.

Publisher and collector

John Ruskin's publisher, George Allen (1832–1907) was an avid mineral collector. He obtained samples from the Stowe collection of the 1st Duke of Buckingham and Chandos sold in 1848; from the Cornish mineral dealer Richard Talling; and from Ruskin himself. Over 1,400 of his specimens are now in the Museum.

George Allen's notebook and one of his agates

Copper ore is made into wire and pipes

Moss agate snuff box

Beautiful and useful

Humans are sometimes defined as tool-making animals: our early ancestors made an important cultural advance when they realised that the Earth on which they lived contained materials that could make their life easier. We are also a species that appreciates the beauty of our material resources.

Noticing that some rocks were harder than others was a first step towards making flint tools that could hold a sharp edge. Around 4,000 years ago Bronze Age technology reached Britain, as our ancestors smelted ores of copper and tin to make metal weapons, buckles or drinking cups. Today we quarry pure quartz sands to make silicon chips, uranium minerals for nuclear power stations and ores of rare earth metals for lasers.

Whoever buried the 'Red Lady of Paviland' (see p. 31) honoured his bones by colouring them with red ochre, rich in iron oxide minerals. We have been wearing gold jewellery for more than 6,000 years. But our love affair with personal adornment really took off when jewellers discovered how to cut precious stones into facets so that they sparkled in the light. As well as being beautiful, gem minerals are hard and extremely durable and so are useful for such things as dentists' drills.

The Museum's displays illustrate how dependent we are on minerals for many everyday materials.

Which minerals keep us looking good?

Fluorite for fluoride in toothpaste

Zeolites to soften water in washing powder

Corundum for emery boards to file our nails

Talc for talcum powder and make-up

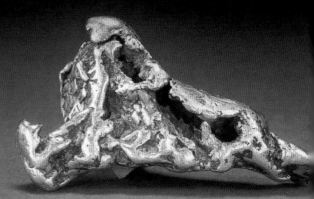

Native gold

Sapphire

Heliodor and
goshenite, two
varieties of beryl

Marble mania

Since ancient times the durability
and stunning beauty of marble and
other decorative stones have made
them very desirable as building
materials. In the early 19th century
Faustino Corsi, the Italian authority
on ancient stone, collected 1000
blocks of the polished marble,
granite and other stones employed
in buildings, furniture and
ornamental sculpture since ancient
Roman times. The Corsi collection,
now in the Museum, is one of the
oldest, largest and best studied in
the world. It provides an invaluable
source of reference for anyone
seeking to identify stones used
to decorate buildings and make
artefacts throughout history.

With a grant from the Esmée
Fairbairn Foundation, Museum staff
are working to create a website
for the Corsi collection. With high-
quality photographs and Corsi's
original descriptions (in English)
the site will make the collection
accessible to anyone interested in
archaeology and the decorative arts.

Minerals on display

As its designers intended, the Museum is itself an illustration of the wonders of the natural world. You can see the beauty and usefulness of British decorative rocks in the columns of polished stone that support the arcades around the central court.

MARVELLOUS MINERALS

For an introduction to the extraordinary variety of minerals in the Museum's collection, see the Minerals case in the central aisle of the court. Here you will find a spectacular specimen of sparkling pyrite, sometimes called 'fool's gold' because it has disappointed so many prospectors; delicate salmon-pink 'flowers' of desert rose gypsum; and the white pointed crystals of calcite, among a brilliant range of colours and crystal shapes.

Move south to explore the subject further in the Earth Materials aisle. On low plinths down the centre of the aisle you can let your fingers do the learning with a succession of large 'touchable' exhibits, including the spectacular Nantan meteorite. Cases on the north side of the aisle tell the story of rock and mineral formation in the Earth's crust: how igneous, sedimentary and metamorphic rocks are constantly recycled from one type to another under the forces of fire and water and the constant movement of the tectonic plates. Rock samples around the southern edges of the court illustrate this never-ending story.

The cases on the south side of the Earth Materials aisle illustrate the way we have interacted with our mineral heritage. Here you will discover the techniques we use to find out about their properties, from looking at them with a simple hand lens to subjecting them to X-ray diffraction. Two cases of British minerals show rare and beautiful specimens, exposed through our rich history of mining for ores of tin, lead and iron. Many of these are no longer available as mines have closed and flooded.

Upstairs in the north east corner of the upper arcade is a display of gemstones, which many might see as the most beautiful of the minerals for their rich colour and sparkle.

(Inset) Plumbogummite from the English Lake District

Touchable gneiss

Rocks from space

100,000 tonnes of extraterrestrial material reach the surface of the Earth every year, but most of it is in the form of tiny particles of dust. Very rarely does a piece of space rock as large as the Museum's Nantan meteorite arrive on Earth. It is one of our 'touchable' exhibits, so you can actually put your hand on something that came from the asteroid belt, a band of rock debris orbiting between Mars and Jupiter. An iron meteorite weighing over 71 kg, it is one of a shower that fell to Earth in China in May 1516, when Henry VIII was King of England.

Crystals that glow in the dark

When they are bathed in ultraviolet radiation, some minerals emit visible light, often in beautiful colours. This is called fluorescence. Lift the heavy curtain over the opening of the enclosed display at the east end of the Earth Materials aisle and you will find yourself in a magical cavern of glowing minerals. The word 'fluorescence' comes from fluorite.

The same specimen in normal light (top) and UV light (bottom)

Thin section of harzburgite under the microscope

Mineralogists at work

The day-to-day work of the Museum's mineralogists involves identifying, cataloguing, conserving and studying our growing collection of rocks and minerals and making them available to students, research scientists and amateur enthusiasts from all over the world. Oxford University is one of five Earth Science Collection Centres that take care of rocks and minerals no longer required at other British universities. As these would be costly to collect in the field, they represent a hugely valuable resource for anyone setting out to do new research.

The collections themselves are historically interesting, some of them dating from early in the 19th century, and curatorial staff are working on archival material relating to the specimens. For example, studying the handwriting and styles of labels can help to build up a picture of the groups or individuals who originally amassed the collections.

A close-up look

The scanning electron microscope is used for researching minerals. It shows crystals at very high magnification, and a detector measures the energy of X-rays emitted when electrons hit the sample, revealing what chemical elements are present.

Above A thin section of staurolite from the Himalayan range reveals when and at what temperature it formed. **Below** Lawrence Wager, and one of his Himalayan specimens.

Lawrence Wager's rocks

Lawrence Wager became Professor of Geology at Oxford in 1950, and his rock collection has remained in the Museum.

In 1933 he was invited to join the British expedition to Mount Everest, where he and a colleague reached a point less than 1,000 feet from the summit. Along the expedition route through Sikkim and southern Tibet he collected 244 rock specimens, among which are some from the ascent route on Everest itself, crossing one of the most significant geological boundaries in the Himalaya.

Limestone near the summit was laid down in an ancient ocean, whereas the rocks at base camp level are sediments deformed, metamorphosed and partly melted deep in the Earth's crust. Recent studies on Wager's Everest specimens reveal the sequence of events and the mechanisms involved in squeezing out a vast, hot slice of the deep crust during the building of the Himalayan range.

oric specimen labels

DIORITE.

214.

The Universe began with a Big Bang around 13.7 billion years ago. Stars formed in clouds of hydrogen and helium, burning these gases and forming heavier elements as a result of nuclear fusion. When they die in supernova explosions, stars expel gas and dust out into space. New stars, including our Sun, are continually forming from interstellar gas and dust, and as discs of cooling debris swirl around them, some of the material clumps together to form planets. One of these is our Earth, but it looked very different at first from the green and blue planet we know today.

The story of the Earth

Position of the continents
250–200 million years ago

For the first 100 million years after its formation 4.54 billion years ago, Earth was red hot and molten from the energy released as it was bombarded by small planets and asteroids. This time in Earth's history is known as the Hadean eon – hell on Earth. One asteroid about the size of Mars made such a powerful impact that it blew into space all the material that eventually formed the Moon. Meanwhile the materials making up the Earth separated into layers. Heavy metallic elements, mostly iron, formed a magnetic core, while a mantle of lighter elements floated above.

An outer crust of rock formed on this molten ball, and eventually the bombardment ceased. Volcanic steam and water from icy comets combined to form a water-rich atmosphere, which eventually filled the Earth's oceans with rain. Between the oceans, continents were gradually built up on crustal plates which moved over the surface of the mantle, reaching positions approximating to those we recognise today only a few million years ago.

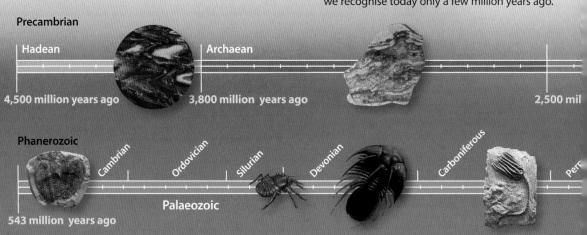

Precambrian

Hadean

Archaean

4,500 million years ago

3,800 million years ago

2,500 mil

Phanerozoic

Cambrian

Ordovician

Silurian

Devonian

Carboniferous

Perm

Palaeozoic

543 million years ago

Model Earth in the upper gallery. At only a few miliimetres across, it is on the same scale as the model Sun on the opposite gallery (see p 60)

Boiled, baked and beaten

The intensely hot rocks of the Earth's mantle are constantly circulating, slowly dragging with them the huge plates bearing continents and oceans. Where the edge of a plate sinks into the mantle, parts of the rock above melt away to form magma. When hot magma rises to be trapped inside the crust or erupted from volcanoes, it cools, and crystals of minerals grow to form new rocks.

Over the Earth's 4.5 billion year history, plate movements have buried rocks and raised them up, causing great changes in temperature and pressure that have forged one form of rock into another, time and time again – a process known as metamorphism. Hot water carried by this constantly stirring chemical stewpot can dissolve away some minerals and deposit new ones. Rivers, seas, ice and rain can all break down a rock, and where the fragments collect together, a new one forms. The composition and structure of each rock holds within it the story of its formation.

The plates are still moving: earthquakes result when energy is suddenly released as plates grind against one another along the fault between them.

The Earth is constantly changing, as continents and oceans shift, ice sheets advance and retreat, volcanoes erupt and the occasional asteroid collides. The story is told in the rocks, which have been repeatedly heated, cooled, compressed, eroded and redeposited over millions of years. From the middle Precambrian onwards, creatures fossilised within the layers of rock begin to tell a new story – the story of life.

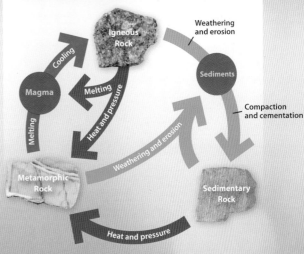

Igneous Rock

Weathering and erosion

Cooling

Sediments

Magma

Melting

Compaction and cementation

Melting

Heat and pressure

Weathering and erosion

Metamorphic Rock

Sedimentary Rock

Heat and pressure

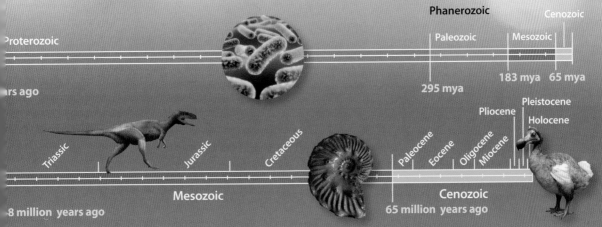

Phanerozoic

Cenozoic

Paleozoic

Mesozoic

Proterozoic

183 mya   65 mya

295 mya

...rs ago

Pliocene

Pleistocene

Holocene

Paleocene

Eocene

Oligocene

Miocene

Triassic

Jurassic

Cretaceous

Mesozoic

Cenozoic

8 million years ago

65 million years ago

Geology is the study of the materials that make up the Earth, including the fossilised remains of living things, and how they change over time. In our Museum we have a separate collection of rocks and minerals, so the Geological Collections consist chiefly of fossils. When the Museum first opened, fossil collecting was both a serious area of enquiry and a popular hobby, as it has remained ever since.

Fabulous fossils

Spectacular skeletons of *Iguanodon* and *Tyrannosaurus* greet you as you enter the Museum. These are casts of fossil specimens found over a century ago in Belgium, and more recently in South Dakota, USA, confirming that there was once a time when dinosaurs ruled the Earth. But our planet teemed with life long before the dinosaurs arrived. You will find abundant examples of extraordinary creatures in our displays, some of them over 550 million years old. Specimens such as these provided the first evidence for the great age of the Earth and the evolution of life upon it.

Oxford's Geological Collections contain around half a million fossils. They include specimens collected and described by Edward Lhwyd, the second Keeper of the old Ashmolean Museum, in the 17th century, and by Sir Charles Lyell, the author of *Principles of Geology* (1830–32), who was one of the first to argue that the Earth was much older than biblical scholars suggested. Among a collection of fossil dinosaur remains from Oxfordshire are bones from the *Megalosaurus* described by William Buckland in 1824, the first of the giant prehistoric reptiles to be scientifically recorded. Buckland's 'Red Lady', the oldest anatomically modern human fossil skeleton in the UK, is also on display in the Museum.

Both professional geologists and enthusiastic local amateurs continue to collect wherever road building or quarrying exposes promising strata. Recent discoveries include the pliosaur skeleton recovered from a claypit near the Oxfordshire village of Yarnton in 1994, quantities of Jurassic ammonites and other marine invertebrates exposed as the M40 motorway sliced through this county, and extraordinary soft-bodied fossils from Herefordshire.

Smith's geological map of Oxfordshire

Buckland's *Megalosaurus* jaw

William Smith, the 'Father of Geology'

William Smith (1769–1839) was the son of a blacksmith, born in the village of Churchill in Oxfordshire. Through his work as a surveyor for canals, he noticed that rocks in Britain came in many different types, and that the same types could be found in many different places. He established for the first time that these surface rocks represented strata that had been laid down on top of one another over very long periods of time and subsequently re-exposed. He also proposed that the fossils found within the strata could help to determine their sequence, and made the first geological map of the country, published in 1815. The Museum's archives hold a collection of his earliest maps, and his correspondence with scientific colleagues.

Edward Lhwyd's catalogue

Edward Lhwyd (1660–1709) was the second Keeper of the old Ashmolean Museum, holding the post from 1691 until his death in the Museum in 1709. He was an indefatigable collector of fossils, and prepared a catalogue of 1766 beautifully-drawn specimens that was published in 1699. The subjects of sixteen of his drawings, including the tooth of a great white shark, can be clearly identified among the Museum's collections, which makes them the oldest documented fossil specimens from Britain. Lhwyd was puzzled to find so many fossils of sea creatures buried on land. He suggested that 'seeds' of marine animals were drawn up into mists that drifted over the land; he thought that these 'seeds' then burrowed into the rock and germinated underground.

Shark's teeth from Lhwyd's catalogue, and one of his real specimens

What is a fossil?

Fossils are the remains of animals or plants that were once alive. Today's animals and plants have evolved from some of the fossilised species we find in rocks. Many animals decay and leave no trace when they die. Others become buried in mud on the sea floor. Over millions of years the mud turns to rock around the hard parts of the animal. Minerals then take up the space of the skeleton or shell and form a perfect cast. Long afterwards this fossil comes to the surface again.

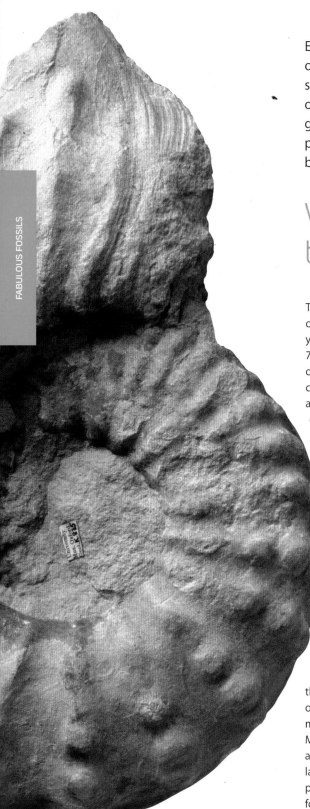

Everyone is interested in the story of our origins. It is written, over billions of years, in the succession of rocks that form the Earth under our feet. The chapters of that story are the groups of animals and plants that occupied our planet over the ages and whose remains have been frozen in time as fossils.

Written in the rock

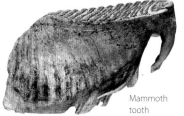

Mammoth tooth

The first, very long chapter, is all about tiny, single-celled organisms that lack a nucleus. First appearing about 3.5 billion years ago, these were the only form of life on Earth for at least 750 million years. Some left signs of their presence in the form of stromatolites, rocky formations built by communities of cyanobacteria. Organisms with cells that had nuclei began to appear about 1.45 billion years ago. From these, true multi-cellular organisms arose, leading to an explosion in the number of species living in the ocean and later on land.

Life continued to evolve, surviving five major extinction events. The most dramatic was at the end of the Permian period, just over 250 million years ago, when over 90% of species became extinct. Each time, new species arose and reoccupied the Earth. The fossil record allows us to trace this process and ask questions about the greening of the land, the dominance of the dinosaurs, or the first appearance of birds and mammals.

These questions are relevant to us today as we contemplate a world that is warming. The fossil record tells us how our environment has changed in the past. At different times Oxfordshire has been under the sea, warm enough to support lions and their prey, and close to the edge of the Arctic ice sheet. Studying fossil communities, or palaeoecology, can help us to understand how modern species might respond to similar challenges. Museum collections are vital as building and other changes in land use close off the possibility of digging for more specimens.

Lion's jawbone from Oxfordshire

Cretaceous ammonite

Fossil fuels

Oil and natural gas have formed over millions of years from the decayed remains of plankton that once lived in the oceans. Coal is derived from decomposed land plants that in Britain derive from the Carboniferous period. Geologists have helped the oil and coal mining industries to locate deposits of these fossil fuels. We still depend on them for most of our energy, although we recognise that these sources are non-renewable, and that burning them is leading to an increase in the concentration of carbon dioxide in the atmosphere.

The Earth is very old

If you could compress the Earth's 4.5 billion year history into a single year, the first animals with hard parts such as shells would not appear until almost the end of November. The dinosaurs would die out the day after Christmas, and humans like us would finally turn up just after 11.35 pm on 31 December. Your whole life would pass in little more than half a second!

Stromatolite

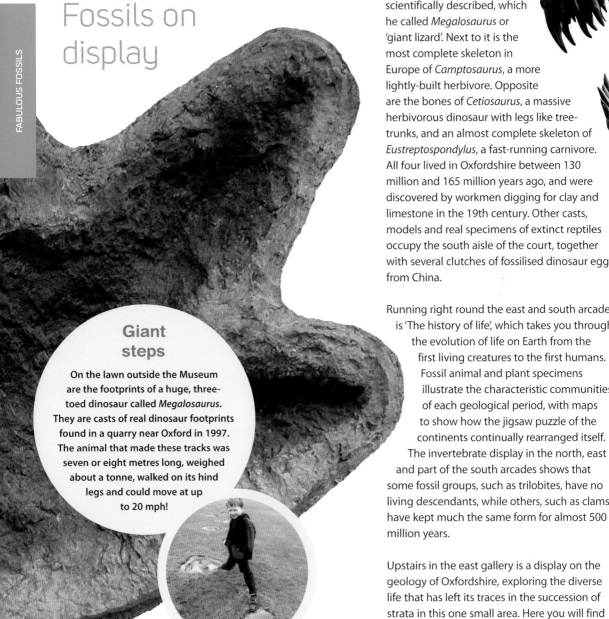

Young visitors will want to start with the dinosaurs, which take centre stage in the court. But a tour round the fossil displays will take you to almost every part of the Museum.

Fossil coral from Oxfordshire

Fossils on display

Walk down the centre aisle, with the casts of *Iguanodon* and *Tyrannosaurus* skeletons towering above you. On the left you will come to cases celebrating the great geologist William Buckland and his astonishing discovery, the first dinosaur to be scientifically described, which he called *Megalosaurus* or 'giant lizard'. Next to it is the most complete skeleton in Europe of *Camptosaurus*, a more lightly-built herbivore. Opposite are the bones of *Cetiosaurus*, a massive herbivorous dinosaur with legs like tree-trunks, and an almost complete skeleton of *Eustreptospondylus*, a fast-running carnivore. All four lived in Oxfordshire between 130 million and 165 million years ago, and were discovered by workmen digging for clay and limestone in the 19th century. Other casts, models and real specimens of extinct reptiles occupy the south aisle of the court, together with several clutches of fossilised dinosaur eggs from China.

Running right round the east and south arcades is 'The history of life', which takes you through the evolution of life on Earth from the first living creatures to the first humans. Fossil animal and plant specimens illustrate the characteristic communities of each geological period, with maps to show how the jigsaw puzzle of the continents continually rearranged itself. The invertebrate display in the north, east and part of the south arcades shows that some fossil groups, such as trilobites, have no living descendants, while others, such as clams, have kept much the same form for almost 500 million years.

Upstairs in the east gallery is a display on the geology of Oxfordshire, exploring the diverse life that has left its traces in the succession of strata in this one small area. Here you will find tributes to William Smith and other prominent Oxford geologists: Robert Plot, Edward Lhwyd, William Buckland and Joscelyn Arkell.

Giant steps

On the lawn outside the Museum are the footprints of a huge, three-toed dinosaur called *Megalosaurus*. They are casts of real dinosaur footprints found in a quarry near Oxford in 1997. The animal that made these tracks was seven or eight metres long, weighed about a tonne, walked on its hind legs and could move at up to 20 mph!

Cast of *Tyrannosaurus rex* skeleton

Hand tools

As the city of Oxford developed
during the 19th century, the
surrounding area was excavated
for clay, limestone and gravel to
make bricks and build roads. The
labourers doing the digging soon
discovered that they were not the
first to be working on those sites.
They turned up dozens of flint hand
axes, made between
200,000 and 400,000
years ago by *Homo
erectus*, one of the
predecessors of
modern humans.
The workmen had
the good sense to
supplement their
pay by selling
their finds to
museums.

The 'Red Lady'

In 1823 William Buckland
was digging in a cave in the
limestone cliffs on the Gower
Peninsula in South Wales when
he discovered a human skeleton.
It was coloured with red ochre
and buried with ornaments
of shell and ivory. As he had
no idea of humanity's ancient
origins, Buckland tentatively
suggested that the skeleton
belonged to a woman from the
Roman occupation of Britain,
around the first century AD.
We now know that the body
is of a young man aged about
21, and that he lived 29,000
years ago, before the last Ice
Age. His is the oldest fossil
skeleton of an anatomically
modern human ever found
in the UK: casts of the bones
are on display to protect the
original specimen.

Geologists at work

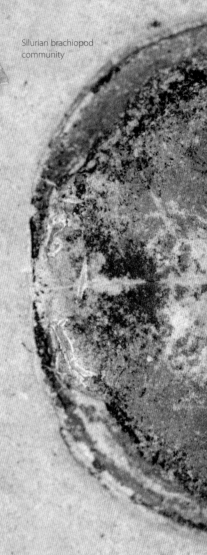

Silurian brachiopod community

Having survived for many millions of years, most fossils do not present curators with a conservation problem. The Museum's geologists focus their attention on completing the cleaning, classification, description and cataloguing of their large and diverse holdings. These descriptions go beyond the size and shape of individual specimens to include fossil communities and the environments in which they were found, as well as the relationship between species and their positions on the tree of life.

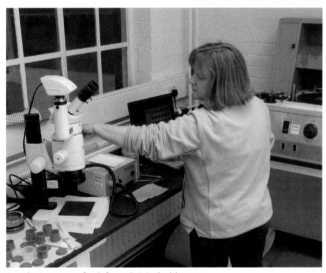

A geologist prepares fossils for analysis in the laboratory

Oxford's collection is rich in assemblages of marine invertebrates with hard shells, such as brachiopods or lamp shells, that date from the Cambrian period onwards. Since the 1960s brachiopods have been used to work out the relative depths in the ancient oceans at which various species and communities lived. The changing sequence of these species in a rock section therefore indicates the times during geological history when the sea level has risen and fallen. These principles, first applied to Silurian rocks and fossils in the Welsh borders, have now been extended to strata of many other time periods and in many regions of the world.

Crustacean from the Chengjiang fossil deposit

Survival of the softest

In extremely rare, very special locations around the world, organisms have been preserved with all their soft parts intact, including some of the earliest animals in the fossil record. One of the most extraordinary examples is in Chengjiang, Yunnan Province, China. In 2010 the Museum collaborated with Chinese geologists to exhibit some 130 fossil specimens, including a fish that is the earliest known vertebrate, during our anniversary year.

'Virtual fossil' of a sea spider from Herefordshire

The Oxford pliosaur

The Jurassic Oxford Clay is rich in fossil remains, and collectors are used to coming home with interesting finds. One of the most exciting was unearthed by a sharp-eyed curator from the Museum in 1994, who spotted part of a jaw sticking out from the side of a clay pit near the Oxfordshire village of Yarnton, only a few metres from the main road. With the help of the company digging the pit, a team from the Museum carefully removed the almost-complete skeleton of a pliosaur. The animal was a sea-dwelling, carnivorous reptile 3 metres long, with jaws like a crocodile and large, paddle-like limbs. More than 20 years later the painstaking process of clearing the compacted clay from the fossil bones still continues: as they are liberated from the rock they are added to the skeleton, on display in the court as it was found.

Closer to home, exceptionally preserved fossils occur in 425-million-year-old Silurian rocks in Herefordshire. It is impossible to remove these delicate fossils from their surrounding matrix of rock, and initially they could be seen only as two-dimensional traces on a split surface. Geologists at the Museum have taken a bold decision to use computer reconstruction to reveal the full glory of these ancient creatures – destroying the fossils themselves in the process. The method involves grinding the rock that contains the fossil a fraction of a millimetre at a time and photographing each layer as it is revealed. The computer is then used to create a composite 'virtual fossil' image from the photographs, which the scientists can colour to distinguish particular body parts, and which they can view and investigate in 3-D on screen.

Did you know...

...that many years ago, people who found ammonites thought that they were coiled snakes that had been turned to stone? Now we know that they are extinct, sea-living animals related to modern squid. Other common fossils, related to snails, are called 'devil's toenails'.

Classifying animals and plants is fundamental to the study of the living world. People who specialise in assigning species to groups are called taxonomists. Taxonomy is an important part of the work of natural history museums: ours holds many 'type specimens' that are the reference points for their species.

The tree of life

Traditionally, taxonomists work by minutely comparing one specimen with another: measuring bodies, counting hairs or appendages, looking at the structure of teeth or shells. Modern taxonomy also makes use of DNA analysis where enough animal or plant tissue is available. Another area of study, called phylogenetics, works out relationships both between living creatures, and between those alive today and their extinct ancestors.

The 18th-century Swedish biologist Carl Linnaeus first established the hierarchical system of organising the natural world into kingdoms, classes, orders, families, genera and species, using a method of classification based on shared physical characteristics. Because they shared similar characters, he put humans alongside monkeys and apes in the order Primates.

In 1859 Charles Darwin published his book *On the Origin of Species by Means of Natural Selection*. He proposed that living species had evolved from ancient ancestors that might have looked quite different. Darwin suggested that the similarities between species reflected their common ancestry, and that differences came about through environmental factors influencing the survival and reproduction of individuals with different adaptations. He used the metaphor of the 'Tree of Life' to show how a common root in the distant past could have given rise to many branches.

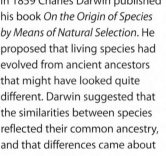

Fungi

Animals

Archaebacteria

Plants

True bacteria

Eucaryotes

Life

The animals are just one of the many branches on the tree of life. Of animal species, 95% are invertebrates (animals without a backbone, such as insects, snails and shrimps). The remaining 5% are vertebrates: fish, amphibians, reptiles, birds and mammals, which include our own species, *Homo sapiens*.

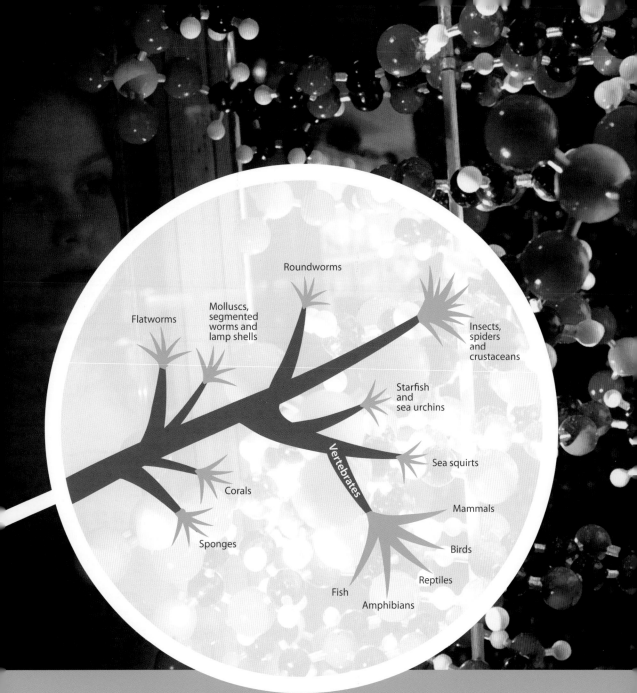

Roundworms

Molluscs, segmented worms and lamp shells

Flatworms

Insects, spiders and crustaceans

Starfish and sea urchins

Sea squirts

Vertebrates

Corals

Mammals

Sponges

Birds

Reptiles

Fish

Amphibians

The double helix of DNA

Darwin's theory of evolution by natural selection is the most powerful idea in modern biology. It explains almost everything we see in the living world: the peacock's tail, the giraffe's long neck, or food-sharing among chimpanzees. But even Darwin did not know what was the underlying mechanism that enabled new characteristics to become established. The first clue to patterns of inheritance came from the Bohemian monk Gregor Mendel's 19th century studies of pea plants. But it was not until 1953 that James Watson and Francis Crick discovered the double helix of DNA, and we at last understood how small genetic changes from one generation to another can lead to new adaptations. Eventually, groups of animals that evolve new adaptations in separate habitats may no longer be able to interbreed, and so become distinct species.

The skeletons of large animals, such as whales and giraffes, are among the most spectacular exhibits in the Museum. But they represent only a tiny fraction of the specimens in the Zoological Collections, which range from large mammals and birds all the way down to models of single-celled organisms.

Amazing animals

Black capped kingfisher

Our 500,000 or so specimens include historically important objects such as the crabs that Charles Darwin collected during the voyage of the *Beagle* in 1831–36, and the only known dodo remains that include skin as well as bone. An actively-growing collection of shrimps is helping to map the diversity of the underwater world.

During the early days of the Museum, Darwin's theory of evolution by natural selection spurred naturalists to study the variations and special adaptations of animal species. Specimens in the Museum illustrate the full range of the animal kingdom: mammals, birds, reptiles, amphibians, fish, and invertebrates (which are by far

Arowana, a primitive ray-finned fish

the most numerous). They have been preserved in many forms: stuffed and mounted, as partial or complete skeletons, pickled in spirit or stored as dried skins. Birds' eggs, nests and pellets help to tell their whole life story. The collection also includes models in glass, wax or plaster that were made as teaching aids.

As is true of all the collections, many more specimens are carefully stored in cabinets for research and teaching than are on display. Here in the Museum, 19th century anatomy students would dissect many species of animal as they learned how the forms of limbs, tails or teeth followed from the function they had to perform, while bones and organs from pathological studies on human subjects were also retained for teaching.

In the 21st century we use specimens to answer questions about the taxonomy, ecology and conservation of animals, and to teach people about evolution and biodiversity. Our historic acquisitions, especially those from wild populations that are now protected, have a value for science at least as great as that of specimens collected more recently.

Seahorse

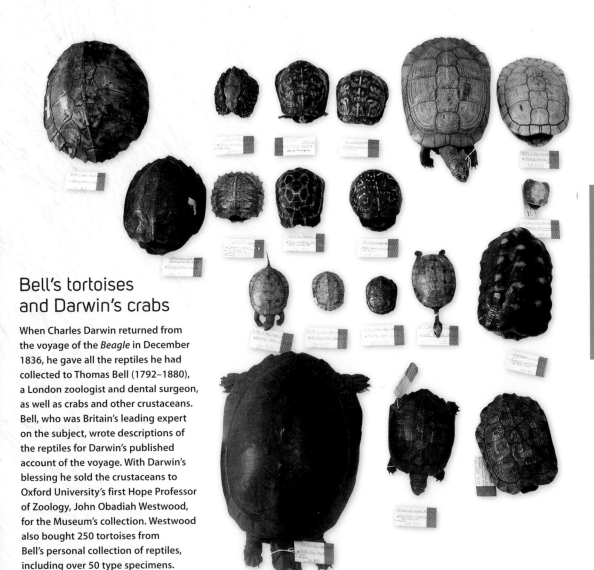

Bell's tortoises and Darwin's crabs

When Charles Darwin returned from the voyage of the *Beagle* in December 1836, he gave all the reptiles he had collected to Thomas Bell (1792–1880), a London zoologist and dental surgeon, as well as crabs and other crustaceans. Bell, who was Britain's leading expert on the subject, wrote descriptions of the reptiles for Darwin's published account of the voyage. With Darwin's blessing he sold the crustaceans to Oxford University's first Hope Professor of Zoology, John Obadiah Westwood, for the Museum's collection. Westwood also bought 250 tortoises from Bell's personal collection of reptiles, including over 50 type specimens.

By wagon through Africa

The naturalist William John Burchell (1781–1863) spent five years travelling in South Africa, and another five in Brazil. He made an extensive collection of plants and animals, including over 500 birds from South Africa alone. Travelling in a wagon drawn by oxen, he kept meticulous notebooks of the specimens he collected, many of them new to science. In 1865 his sister Anna donated his animal specimens to the Museum, together with his old tin trunk and the painting he made of his wagon.

Humans and other animals

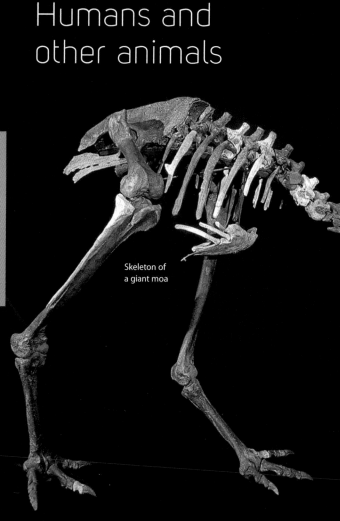

Skeleton of a giant moa

Biodiversity and conservation are important considerations for modern natural history collections. The plight of large and appealing creatures such as tigers and pandas is often in the news, but there are many less glamorous species whose disappearance may do more damage to the diversity of our biosphere. Documenting the evolutionary relationships, location, numbers and genetic make-up of modern populations and comparing them with those of historic specimens can help to build up a picture of how a habitat is changing.

Some of the animals in the Museum's collection no longer exist as living creatures. The most famous example is the dodo, extinct since the 17th century. The Museum also has many bones from the giant moa of New Zealand (extinct in the 14–15th centuries), and specimens of the marsupial thylacine or Tasmanian wolf (extinct since the 1930s). Other animals in the collection, such as the gorilla and the kakapo (a flightless parrot from New Zealand) survive, but are endangered. Each specimen can provide a snapshot of its distribution, ecology and genetics at the time of its collection.

We share the Earth with around 1.25 million other named animal species. But as human populations have grown – from 1 billion in 1800 to nearly 7 billion in 2010 – our increasing 'footprint' has put pressure on our neighbours. Many have been driven to extinction, while others have declined to dangerously small numbers. Extinction is a normal part of the process of evolution, but biologists estimate that species are currently disappearing at 100 to 1,000 times the normal rate as a result of human activity.

Egg of the extinct great auk

The Oxford dodo

There was a stuffed dodo in the Tradescant collection that formed part of the original Ashmolean Museum in the 17th century. Sadly the specimen decayed until there was nothing left but its head and foot. These parts, which include skin as well as bone, are now carefully preserved in the Zoological Collections. In 2003, Oxford researchers were able to extract DNA from the bones and confirm that the dodo is related to pigeons.

The Museum's dodo display in the central aisle now includes a cast of the dodo's head, together with a composite skeleton made up of casts of dodo bones. A reconstruction of the dodo based on modern research has revealed that it was a much more athletic bird than the fat, comical creature depicted in early representations.

A booklet, *The Oxford Dodo*, is available from the Museum shop.

Skin, skull and foot of the Oxford dodo

Dodo reconstruction

The 'skeleton parade' that marches down the north aisle of the court has been a feature of the Museum since its early days. From the lofty giraffe (a survivor from Henry Acland's Christ Church anatomy museum) to the polar bear, they march two by two, their bony structures inviting comparisons both with the dinosaur skeletons nearby and with the arched ribs of the Museum's roof.

Animals on display

Most of the zoology displays are on this side of the court. Next to the skeletons you will find cases illustrating mammals from different regions of the world, while in the adjacent aisle are the reptiles, fish and amphibians.

For the story of Darwin's theory of evolution by natural selection, see the cases in the arcade in the north west corner. Beyond these are cases devoted to the primates, our nearest living relatives. Opposite, in table cases, is displayed the extraordinary diversity of the invertebrate world in both living and fossil forms: sea urchins, snails, shellfish, squid, crabs and lobsters.

The display of British birds, which has been completely redesigned and opened in 2011, is on the north side of the upstairs gallery. Here you will find the birds of the British Isles arranged according to their typical habitat, and labelled in traffic-light colours of red, amber and green to show how their numbers have changed in recent decades.

Molluscs in the invertebrate display

Acland's tuna

The beautifully articulated skeleton of a tuna fish has one of the most dramatic histories of any object in the Museum. Henry Acland acquired the huge fish in Madeira in December 1846 for his anatomical collection at Christ Church. But as he was returning home by sea, a storm blew up in the Bay of Biscay. Acland had to open his coffin-shaped box to persuade the sailors that it did not contain a human corpse: blaming it for the storm, they were about to throw it overboard.

The ship sailed on but was wrecked off the Dorset coast, and passengers and crew had to struggle to shore in small boats. The sailors saved the precious fish, and it arrived in Oxford in perfect condition. The tuna skeleton in its glass case was one of the first exhibits to go on display when the Museum opened in 1860 – together with a Latin inscription about its adventures that was mercilessly parodied by Charles Dodgson (Lewis Carroll) and his friends.

Lewis Carroll and the Museum

Charles Dodgson was a mathematics don at Christ Church who befriended the Dean's daughters Alice, Edith and Lorina Liddell. As soon as the Museum opened they became frequent visitors, and Dodgson would make up stories about the animals on display. The Museum specimens undoubtedly provided the models for characters such as the Dodo in *Alice's Adventures in Wonderland*, which Dodgson wrote under the name Lewis Carroll. A display in the centre aisle of the court illustrates the Carroll connection.

The taxidermist's art

Stuffed animals and birds were once regarded as works of decorative art as well as natural history specimens. In glass cases around the north side of the court are many examples of exotic birds mounted as the taxidermist thought they might look in life. The crow family is a favourite, and visitors often pause to wonder at the lightness of the sand grouse in flight.

In the storage rooms behind the scenes are walls hung with horns and antlers, drawers full of bird skins with their brilliant feathers, bottles of body parts, and boxes of bones.

Zoologists at work

Like the other collections, Zoology has a backlog of work simply to record what it holds and make it accessible to researchers. The routine work includes protecting specimens from pests or other forms of decay, preparing them for exhibition, identifying bones, eggshells and other finds for members of the public, answering requests for loans, and teaching students. New acquisitions from most animal groups are infrequent these days, but we continue to add to the scientific collection of marine invertebrates.

The Zoological Collections have made it possible, among other questions, to clear up confusion about the gender and species of specimens of the extinct moa, by analysing DNA from bones, and to present cut marks on the bones of giant lemurs as evidence that hunting by humans contributed to their extinction.

In search of shrimps

The shrimp collection, stored in spirit in glass jars, is the most actively growing within the Zoological Collections. Shrimps are among the oldest forms of complex life on Earth: fossil shrimps have been found in rocks from around 200 million years ago. Today there are around 3,500 species known, but there could be as many still undiscovered. They have adapted to an extraordinary variety of environments, from freshwater ponds to hydrothermal vents 2 km down in the deep ocean.

Many undersea habitats, such as coral reefs, are endangered, and shrimps form an important part of these communities. The Museum's collection currently includes about a quarter of the world's total of species, and every collecting trip brings back new ones. Each must be minutely studied to ascertain its place in the shrimp family tree, using both the time-honoured taxonomist's skill of comparative anatomy and more modern techniques that involve reading and comparing sequences of DNA. The Museum's expertise in this area has made a major contribution to our current understanding of the classification of all known living and extinct shrimps.

Body and spirit

Museum specimens have been preserved in 'spirit of wine' (alcohol) since the 17th century. The Museum has examples from 300 years of anatomical study, some of whole animals, others of carefully dissected limbs or organs preserved for teaching. The process bleaches the specimens to a ghostly whiteness, against which blood vessels or bones were sometimes dyed to make them stand out. A recent grant made it possible to carry out conservation work on the spirit collections, making sure that the jars were securely sealed, checking dates and labels, and shelving them in a new storage system.

The Piltdown hoax

In 1912 Charles Dawson and colleagues claimed to have found the skull of an early human in a gravel pit in East Sussex. It appeared to be a 'missing link', with a human cranium but an ape-like jaw. In 1953 the Oxford anatomist Joseph Weiner exposed 'Piltdown Man' as the biggest fake in this history of anthropology, put together from human and orangutan remains.

The piece of orangutan jawbone he used for comparison then lay unnoticed with a cast of 'Piltdown Man's' jaw in the Department of Human Anatomy for more than half a century. Their historic significance was recognised only recently when the department gave the bones to the Museum as part of a clear-out of unwanted teaching specimens.

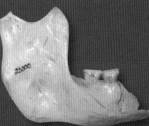

Armed with butterfly nets and festooned with collecting tins, the naturalists of the 18th and 19th centuries were determined to make sense of the bewildering variety of the insect world. The Museum's Entomology Collections date from this period.

Incredible insects

Beetles make up the largest group of insects, but butterflies, moths, bees, wasps, ants, termites, flies, fleas, bugs, grasshoppers, crickets, dragonflies and lice are also insects (count the legs – they all have six). Insects are the most diverse and successful group of animals on Earth. Over a million species have been described to date, making up more than three quarters of all known animal species, and entomologists find many more each year.

Within the Hope Entomological Collections you will also find arachnids (spiders, mites and scorpions) and myriapods (centipedes and millipedes). All are arthropods, meaning that they have jointed legs and a hard external skeleton.

Here in the Hope Collections, 27,500 drawers hold over 5 million specimens, each neatly pinned and labelled with the name of the person who collected it, and the date and place it was found. Over 25,000 of these are type specimens – those from which the species was first described. They include specimens collected by pioneering naturalists such as Charles Darwin and Alfred Russel Wallace. The world's oldest pinned insect, a Bath White butterfly collected around 1702, is only one of many historically important specimens in the Museum.

The collection is used mainly for research in taxonomy, ecology and evolution, and is an invaluable source of reference for biologists from all over the world.

Not all creepy-crawlies are insects

Which of these are not insects?
a) Spider   b) Wasp   c) Beetle
d) Woodlouse   e) Ladybird

a) and d) are not insects.

There are 1.25 million known animal species on Earth – 75% of these are insects

Bath white butterfly

Hope conquers all

The Reverend Frederick William Hope (1797–1862) began collecting beetles as a student at Oxford and went on to become one of the foremost entomologists of his time, using his considerable wealth to buy specimens from all over the world. Many naturalists, including Charles Darwin, also gave him their finds. In 1849 he presented his entire insect collection to Oxford University on condition that it was properly cared for, and it remains the foundation of the Hope Entomological Collections. Hope's donation also included his extensive collection of entomological books, which forms part of the Museum's important reference library.

You can download a history of the collections from www.oum.ox.ac.uk/collect/entom.htm.

Insects are not only the most diverse, but also the most numerous animals on Earth. They play a number of significant roles in all ecosystems, from your back garden (or your kitchen cupboard) to the tropical rainforests of the Amazon. You might not be a fan of 'creepy crawlies', but the Museum's displays will give you a new respect for their versatility.

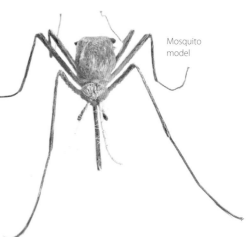
Mosquito model

Living with insects

Insects are a crucial part of the food webs that sustain ecosystems. They provide food for birds and many other creatures great and small; they prey on other insects and keep their numbers in check; and they are among Nature's rubbish disposal experts, recycling nutrients as they munch through plant and animal waste.

Many flying insects collect nectar from flowering plants, brushing against the pollen-heavy stamens as they do so and carrying the pollen grains on their bodies from one plant to another. While we enjoy the profusion of colourful flowers that has evolved to attract insects, pollinators have a serious economic role to play in ensuring that plants produce fruit as well as flowers. Without insect pollinators there would be little left to grow for food apart from cereal crops. Bees are among the most important crop pollinators, so it is particularly worrying that both honey bees and bumblebees have been in decline for the past few decades, probably due to the combined effects of disease, careless use of agricultural pesticides and loss of habitat as agriculture has become more intensive.

We couldn't live without insects, but some of them are a threat. Pests such as locusts or weevils can have a devastating effect on food production. Infectious diseases such as malaria or dengue fever cause millions of deaths in the developing world, and are carried by biting insects such as mosquitoes.

Encouraging beneficial insects and controlling pests depends on understanding their ecology and studying changes in their genetics or habitat. The Hope Entomological Collections are a vital resource for such studies, as their holdings illustrate the historical distribution of insect species, and many of their specimens are available for genetic analysis.

Insects are important plant pollinators

Did you know...

...that one of the biggest headaches for insect curators is an insect? Dead, dried insects are the favourite food of a beetle called *Anthrenus* that just loves living where people live. As well as eating plant, animal and insect specimens in museums, its larvae (known as 'woolly bears') eat wool carpets, fluff and fabric in our homes. Finding the resources to move the rest of our priceless collections safely into pest-proof cabinets is one of the biggest challenges for the Museum's entomologists.

Livingstone's tsetse fly

The African explorer David Livingstone had to contend with many species of biting insect as he trekked across the savannah of Nyasaland (now Malawi) in the 1850s. He caught these specimens of *Glossina morsitans* and sent them to John Obadiah Westwood, the first Curator of the Hope Entomological Collections, who named this and two other species of tsetse fly. Later Hope Professors have worked on the impact of tsetse as the carrier of trypanosomiases – diseases including sleeping sickness in humans and 'nagana' in domestic animals.

Insects on display

Because the insect specimens are so fragile, most of them are kept in specially-designed cabinets in one of several storage rooms. The main entomology displays for visitors to the Museum are on the south side of the upper gallery.

At the top of the stairs is a case illustrating the wonderful diversity of the insect world. In the room immediately to your right is the Museum's beehive, in a specially-designed case that reveals all the activities of the colony (including the famous waggle dance) and allows the bees to come and go freely through an opening in the window frame. Leaving the beehive room, turn right and then right again along the south gallery. The wall cases walk you through the insect orders one by one, using photographs, models and specimens to illustrate the forms and lifestyles of insects from all over the world, from body lice to butterflies.

On the opposite side of the same gallery, a series of themed table cases illustrate the importance of insects in the world. Here you can learn all about insects as pollinators, disease vectors, household and agricultural pests and even as food. You can discover the important roles that insects play in your garden, and see how they have become part of the landscape of popular culture, even as many of them are threatened with extinction through the loss of their habitats.

Master builders

Most people today would call the pest control officer in if they found a wasps' nest in their house. But when in 1857 Mr S. Stone of Brighthampton discovered a 12 cm nest of *Vespula germanica* in the grounds of Cokethorpe Park in Oxfordshire, he brought it indoors and hung it near a window. Supplied with a daily diet of sugar and beer, the wasps expanded their beautifully-constructed nest to a diameter of over half a metre.

Alive and wriggling

In addition to the millions of dried and pinned specimens, the entomology staff keep a small menagerie of live insects and spiders. Living in specially-constructed glass terraria you will find Madagascan hissing cockroaches, giant millipedes, stick insects, some large beetles and a salmon-pink tarantula. On special occasions some of them come out to be introduced to visitors, who are able to handle them and get a really close look.

Beetlemania

Beetles are the diversity champions: entomologists have discovered 450,000 species and more are turning up all the time. They make up 40% of known insect species, and around a quarter of all known life-forms. No wonder that the biologist J.B.S. Haldane (1892–1964), when he was asked what the works of Creation told him about the mind of the Creator, replied 'An inordinate fondness for beetles'.

Entomologists at work

Like a beehive, the entomology collection is always busy. The collection is very large and the specimens very fragile, and like the other collections it has only a small staff to take care of it.

For a long time resources were too stretched to make all this material easily accessible to scholars – even the staff did not know exactly what they had. At the same time the Victorian storage cabinets fell prey to pests and the priceless collections within them were threatened. Since the mid-1980s the curatorial staff have been working systematically to organise, catalogue and rehouse the collections so that they are safe from pests and accessible to members of the public who want to study them. Volunteers are doing much of this work, under the careful supervision of the Museum staff. While it might sound dull, the work is constantly throwing up new discoveries, and each has a story behind it.

At the same time the task of documenting the world's disappearing habitats never ends. Collecting expeditions bring back thousands of species every year, some new to science, all of which need to be described to provide a snapshot of their ecology and habitat. This provides an invaluable reference point for scientists all over the world, and particularly in the countries where the animals originated.

Every year staff respond to requests to borrow specimens, sending out around 8,000 that can be studied alongside examples from other collections. They also answer up to 1,000 enquiries, and look after the many visitors who come to work on the material in Oxford.

Bug quest

Do you have an insect you want to identify? There are about 25 groups of insect, but most belong to one of six common groups: beetles, butterflies and moths, wasps, bees and ants, true bugs, flies, or grasshoppers and crickets. Go to www.oum.ox.ac.uk/thezone/insects/instant/index.htm to identify your find and learn more about insects.

Darwin's insects

In 2009, the 200th anniversary of the birth of Charles Darwin, a 16-year-old Oxfordshire schoolgirl called Julia Richards was working in the Museum as part of the Nuffield Bursary Scheme. Julia was examining insects in the original Hope Collection, looking for those that had been collected by Darwin. Darwin and Hope wrote many letters to each other, and these and other letters made it clear that he had given Hope many insect specimens. But the only way to find them was to look at the tiny labels on hundreds of thousands of pinned insects. Julia's persistence paid off – she found no fewer than 128 insect specimens collected by Darwin, some with labels in his own handwriting, including a magnificent iridescent green dung beetle that he acquired during the voyage of the *Beagle*.

Dung beetles from Borneo

There are more than 5,000 species of dung beetle: they perform a useful service by recycling animal dung and returning nutrients to the soil. In rainforest areas their numbers can reflect the abundance of the mammals whose dung they eat. The assistant curator of entomology has been working with another Oxford scientist to monitor dung beetle numbers in Borneo, where fragments of forest are being preserved in areas that are due to be felled for palm oil plantations. They have been able to collect specimens before logging took place, and hope to return later to record any changes.

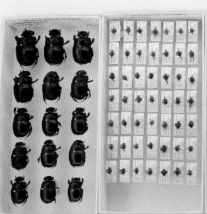

CHARLES DARWIN

The Museum and the community

In 2010 the Museum celebrated its 150th anniversary with a wide range of events and exhibitions. During that year more than half a million visitors passed through its doors.

As recently as 1990, the number of visitors was only 80,000: the Museum saw itself as a predominantly academic institution, opening hours were limited and visitors permitted rather than welcomed. Since the late 1990s there has been a major change in attitude, and the Museum now actively encourages public engagement. Beginning in the year 2000, many of the displays have been extensively redesigned. While still informative for students, the text in these cases aims to engage and inspire curious visitors, rather than to overload them with facts. With its sister museum the Pitt Rivers, the Museum won the Guardian Family Friendly award in 2005, and in 2009 it shared with Oxford University's other museums a Queen's Anniversary Prize for their 'outstanding quality and high public benefit'.

Feeling good!

In 2006 a number of specimens were mounted on plinths or tables without glass cases, and visitors actively invited to touch them. Touchable exhibits include a very popular Shetland pony, a cheetah, dinosaur eggs, a huge slab of fossil trilobites, and some stunning mineral specimens including two meteorites. They are labelled in Braille as well as text so that people with visual impairments can explore them for themselves.

4.6 billion year old meteorite from Argentina

Fun for all

Oxford University's museums work together to encourage enjoyment of the museums in the local community. The Museum runs free, family-friendly activities on Sunday afternoons, when families can borrow a backpack for their visit filled with games, activities and real museum specimens. Additional themed drop-in activities take place during school holidays. A 'Dinosaurs and

Dragon Hunters' afternoon at the Museum of Natural History and the Pitt Rivers attracted record crowds during a dull February half term.

Education staff run free outreach workshops and programmes for community groups, such as a 'Meet the Museums' event with museum specimens, taking the wonder of museums out to groups who might have difficulty making a visit. They also provide tailored sessions within the Museum for groups with special needs, such as learning difficulties or visual impairment.

The main event

The Museum is an enthusiastic participant in city-wide cultural events. On Christmas Light Night it opens its doors until late into the evening, and offers music and Christmas-themed activities to the crowds who fill the streets to see the Christmas lights switched on. It is also a key focus of events for 'Alice's Day', a summer Saturday celebration of Lewis Carroll's characters that embraces the whole city. The annual Oxfordshire Science Festival

features 'Wow! How?', a Saturday when the Museum is filled with 'hands-on' exhibits staffed by enthusiastic young scientists making slime, putting balloons in liquid nitrogen or generating static electricity. 'Oxfordshire Goes Wild' brings local conservation organisations into the museum, introducing visitors to live insects, birds and pond life and encouraging them to promote biodiversity in their local area.

A place for art

The Museum hosts many exhibitions and performances staged by individuals or organisations. Our façade made a striking backdrop to the ten rainforest tree stumps exhibited by Angela Palmer as the 'Ghost Forest' in 2010–12. The front lawn also provided a suitable resting place for the CIAO! (Children's International Art Organisation) Ark Project, an ark made of recycled materials and powered by green energy, exhibiting children's work on the theme of environmental change. Live performances of music and drama transform the Museum, especially at the annual late-night event, 'In A Different Light'.

(Top) The Ciao! Ark on the lawn, June 2010

Wow! How?
at Oxfordshire
Science Festival

During school terms the floor of the Museum is a mosaic of different-coloured uniforms. In 2010 well over 20,000 children visited with their teachers from schools in Oxfordshire and beyond. A further 15,000 overseas students came, many of whom were attending language schools in Oxford.

Tales out of school

A member of the education team greets each party, and guides them through a programme that keeps them not only occupied but entranced during their two-hour visit. The most popular sessions for primary school children are on fossils and dinosaurs; others cover skeletons and minibeasts. Activities include handling exhibits, taking part in workshops and following trails.

Secondary school students benefit from programmes tailored to their exam curricula, and objects in the Geological and Zoological Collections make study days for A level students on evolution and biodiversity memorable. A special study day on 'Life after Darwin' to mark Darwin's bicentenary year in 2009 drew over 250 A level students, who had the opportunity to talk informally to University scientists from professors to graduate students about their research.

'Bug Quest'

A series of 'Bug Quest' projects has helped Oxfordshire primary school students to learn about insects and other 'minibeasts' found in their environment. After training by Museum staff, they set sticky traps in the spring and early summer at chosen locations in their schools. They use keys provided by the Museum to identify trapped specimens; count the numbers of each species; and enter their data in an online spreadsheet which creates graphs and charts of their results. Since the project first ran in 2002, children have found dozens of species including fungus gnats, booklice and a rare purse web spider.

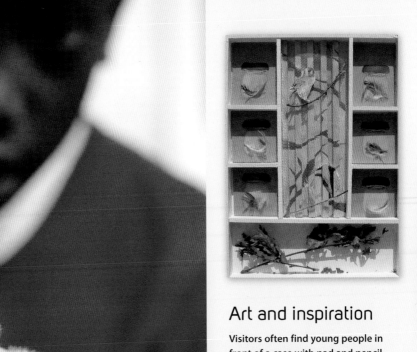

Art and inspiration

Visitors often find young people in front of a case with pad and pencil, absorbed in capturing the balance of a skeleton or the texture of a fossil. The Museum welcomes art students from secondary schools, and offers a range of resources and taught sessions. It also provides a number of online resources jointly with the other museums: see www.museums.ox.ac.uk/arteducation

Local school students' art inspired by the Museum

'"Bug Quest" gives children a chance to take part in a long-term project involving real science. We hope children will be more likely to say "Wow!" and watch the life around them with more interest and enjoyment, than to say "Yuck!" and distance themselves from it.'
Chris Jarvis,
Primary Education Officer

Making museums

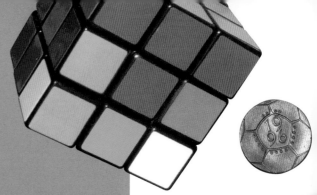

Since 2003 the Museum education staff have run an award-winning outreach project for primary school children with the Pitt Rivers Museum. 'Making Museums' takes children through the whole process of museum curation, from accession to display. In 2010, nearly 1,200 10- and 11-year-olds from schools in East Oxford took part.

Museum education officers visit each class, taking real museum objects – from fossilised dinosaur poo to dreamcatchers. All the children then visit the museums for a whole day and explore what happens in a research collection. They begin by digging up a (plastic!) human skeleton and associated mystery objects, using the museum displays to help identify and classify their finds. Children who are less comfortable with formal book-based learning happily join in with discussion and debate. Finally the children make museums in their classrooms, choosing objects to illustrate aspects of their own lives and deciding how to present them. They proudly show off their exhibits to parents and friends, and education officers visit to see what they have done.

The project was joint winner of the inaugural Clore Award for Museum Learning in 2011.

The Museum of Me

We collect things in museums to help us learn about the world around us through objects. Why not make a museum that tells people about you?

Think about the important things in your life that make up who you are: your family, your friends, the things you enjoy doing, your pets, your school, the place where you live, things you like and don't like.

Decide what kind of objects you want to put in your museum. A photograph of yourself is a good place to start: think about where you want to be photographed and what you might be doing or holding in the photo. Then you can add more photos of your friends and family, pictures cut out of magazines, letters, postcards and birthday cards, or even music. Find some real objects that have special meaning for you: clothes, favourite toys, a football, books or CDs, or natural objects such as stones, shells and leaves that you have collected. You can choose to have a lot of different things, or just a few very special ones.

Now decide how you want to put your collection on display. You can pin pictures to a board, or set your objects out on shelves or in drawers. Try out different ways of arranging them before you decide which is best.

The objects themselves build up a picture of who you are, but you may want to explain more by writing some text to go with them. Notice that in our museum most objects have just a short label giving their names, with a longer piece of writing explaining why the objects in a case are displayed together.

Finally, invite your friends to come and see your museum!

Many of the Museum's visitors come to discover things that they didn't know, see objects they've never seen before and enjoy the building in all its neo-Gothic glory.

The Museum and you

They soon realise that the Museum of Natural History is a fantastic resource that can answer more specific questions. Once you begin to look at the natural world it throws up all sorts of puzzles. If rocks are laid down in horizontal layers, why do the lower levels sometimes come out on top? Why do shrikes have hooked beaks like falcons, when they more closely related to crows? Just how do caterpillars turn into butterflies? A closer look at the Museum exhibits can answer these questions.

Ask an expert

Many people enjoy studying the natural history of their own home regions, or notice different species when they travel on holiday. The Museum's curatorial staff are available to answer scientific enquiries, whether from students and researchers in academic institutions or interested members of the public. You are welcome to bring in rocks, fossils or other finds, or photographs of them, for identification.

Note: The Museum does not condone any illegal actions, such as collecting birds' eggs, trapping live animals or trespassing in quarries or other excavation sites.

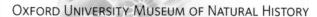

http://www.oum.ox.ac.uk

OXFORD UNIVERSITY MUSEUM OF NATURAL HISTORY

| Home | Visiting Us | Collections & Research | Teaching & Learning | Support the Museum |

The Museum online

The Museum website is the first port of call to find out what special events are planned: www.oum.ox.ac.uk/visiting/whatson.htm. For those who cannot reach the Museum as often as they would like, the website also offers a wealth of online resources suitable for everyone from school children to academic researchers.

'The learning zone' is a collection of interactive pages aimed at young learners, with sections covering the topics of the four main Museum collections: zoology, geology, mineralogy and entomology. It also includes games, puzzles and other fun stuff. See www.oum.ox.ac.uk/thezone

The 'Schools and Teachers' page of the website offers downloadable trails for children to follow as they learn about minerals or minibeasts in the Museum. See www.oum.ox.ac.uk/educate/teachers.htm

The Museum's first online exhibition, 'A few of our favourite things', was created by the staff as part of the 150th anniversary celebrations in 2010, and is at www.oum.ox.ac.uk/favouritethings

'Learning more' is a collection of illustrated documents suitable for older children and adults, covering aspects of the Museum's history, architecture and collections in much more detail than there is room for in this guide. They are free to download at www.oum.ox.ac.uk/learning/index.htm

The catalogues of the four collections are in the process of being entered into electronic databases that are freely accessible online. You can search the databases by species, region, collector or other key words and retrieve details of specimens held in the collections. Some records include illustrations. See www.oum.ox.ac.uk/collect, select the collection you are interested in and click on 'Databases'.

Volunteers

The Museum's packed programme of activities for schools and families is possible only thanks to an army of volunteers who give their time to help children with 'make-and-take' activities, pack backpacks for Family Sundays, or act as stewards at late-night events. They receive training, and find that the experience builds skills and confidence in working with children and the public as well as being very enjoyable. A small number of volunteers also help with curatorial work, such as cleaning and cataloguing specimens. Anyone who is prepared to contribute time to the Museum on a regular basis can register at www.museums.ox.ac.uk/volunteers/register

The Museum and the future

'The Natural History collection of the University requires constant care, special curators, and consequently a considerable annual expenditure... I have therefore to report that I have not sufficient funds at my disposal for carrying out the arrangement of the collections under my care with efficiency or with reasonable promptitude.' So wrote Ray Lankester, Professor of Comparative Anatomy, in the Museum's annual report for 1891. In the ensuing decades successive curators, professors and directors have inevitably echoed his words.

Like all Oxford University's museums, the Museum of Natural History is currently free to visitors, as are all the family and educational activities that it offers. Maintaining the quality of the collections for researchers, improving the experience for visitors, and conserving a glass-roofed building that is more than 150 years old, have required the Museum's custodians to be as inventive as possible when it comes to seeking sources of financial support. In 2010 we launched a £5.5m anniversary fundraising campaign with a dinner on the gallery and a spectacular Son et Lumière.

Grants for the basic running costs of the Museum come from the Higher Education Funding Council for England. From 2003 the work of the Education Department has been funded by *Renaissance*, an

Repairing the roof

Benjamin Woodward's spectacular glass roof leaked almost from the moment it was installed, and it was still leaking in 2010: bright yellow buckets to catch the drips adorned the court every time there was a downpour. After ten years of study and planning, work began in 2011 to repair, replace and clean the exterior tiles. Generous donors have made it possible to use the opportunity to clean and restore the interior painted ironwork and timber to its original 1860 condition.

'The most important work of the museum is invisible to the casual visitor. The research that goes on behind closed doors, the incredible collections – these are the inner heartbeat of the museum.'
Lady Heseltine, Chair of the Advisory Board

initiative of the Museums, Libraries and Archives Council in support of regional museums. Public spending on cultural activities such as museums has always been tight, and became tighter from 2011 as arts and education funding was cut back: at the time of going to press, future income from *Renaissaince* was uncertain.

The Museum is fortunate to have many generous supporters who have enabled it to undertake projects such as the updating of exhibits, the rehousing of vulnerable collections, and the digitising of special holdings such as the Corsi collection of decorative stones. Directors have learned to be alert to opportunities. The dinosaur footprints at Ardley Quarry were revealed when a waste disposal

company, Viridor, was clearing the site. The relationship the company struck up with the Museum through a joint press announcement of the amazing find led Viridor to introduce the Museum to the Landfill Tax Credit Scheme (now the Landfill Communities Fund), grants from which have supported a range of projects.

'We have a responsibility to maintain curation of these internationally significant collections, to protect biological specimens vulnerable to decay, and to exploit them for research. And just as important are the activities for the wider community that are now such an integral part of the Museum's daily life.'
Professor Susan Iversen, Acting Director

How you can help

If you have enjoyed your visit and feel you would like to help us to continue with our work, there are many ways you can do so. The simplest is to place a donation in the collecting box near the main entrance – we suggest £3 per person.

Go shopping!

The Museum shop offers a wonderful selection of toys, gifts and books to suit all pockets. You can buy a cuddly *Stegosaurus*, a real fossil for your collection, or a beautifully-illustrated book on the Museum's architecture. For pocket-money purchasers there are pens, pencils and plastic dinosaurs galore. All the profits go towards the running costs of the Museum. A small selection of items is for sale online at www.oushop.com

Film and TV

Over the years the Museum has featured in *Deadly 60*, *Inspector Morse*, *Walking with Dinosaurs*, *The Lost World* and many other television productions. Staff are happy to provide support for film crews including access to cases, specimens and private rooms.

Steve Backshall of *Deadly 60*

Hire the museum

The Museum is an ideal location for conferences and receptions. The breathtaking neo-Gothic architecture of the main court provides the perfect backdrop for corporate or private entertaining after the doors have closed to the public. The Lecture Theatre is one of the largest in the University; it seats nearly 300 people, and is equipped with state-of-the-art audio-visual equipment. Museum staff can advise you about catering and nearby accommodation. We even have a licence for weddings!

Make a gift that goes further

You can donate to the Oxford University Museum of Natural History via the secure Oxford Thinking website (www.campaign.ox.ac.uk), navigating via 'Find your priority', 'Divisions' and 'Museums'. You can also donate by cheque, made payable to Oxford University Museum of Natural History and sent to the Administrator at the address overleaf. If you are a UK tax-payer, we can claim Gift Aid on your donation and increase its value by almost 30%. Please ask for a Gift Aid declaration to sign.

Legacies can help to secure the future of the Museum and the care of its collections. The value of any gift made to the Museum in your Will is deducted before inheritance tax. If you are interested in making a legacy in favour of a particular area of the Museum's work or wish to leave an object to the collections we would be happy to discuss your wishes with you.

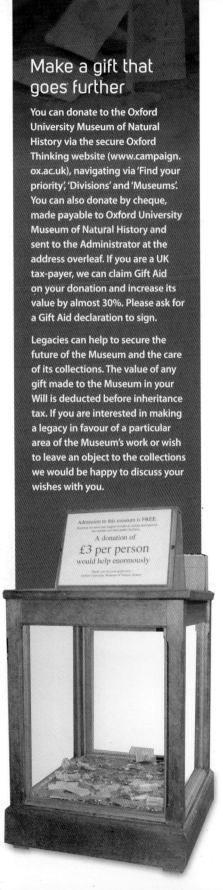

Essential information

Opening hours

At the time of going to press, the Museum is open to visitors from 10.00 until 17.00 every day except over the Christmas and New Year periods and on Easter Sunday. Please check the website for holiday closure dates or any changes to opening hours.

Access

There are disabled parking bays outside the Museum and there is full wheelchair access to all public parts of the building, including a lift to the upper gallery. Disabled toilets are available.

Refreshments

The Museum does not currently have a café. You are welcome to picnic on the lawn outside, but please do not eat or drink in the Museum. The nearest cafés and sandwich shops are in Holywell Street, Broad Street, St Giles and Woodstock Road.

Shop

The shop is open during Museum opening hours and is well stocked with natural history-themed books and gifts.

How to get here

By car: There is no public parking at the Museum, except for disabled visitors. Many Oxford streets are now closed to traffic, and parking in the City of Oxford is severely limited. If coming from outside Oxford, you are strongly recommended to use the excellent Park and Ride buses (see www.oxfordbus.co.uk).

By bus: The Museum is a short walk from stops in Woodstock Road, Banbury Road, Magdalen Street and High Street (see www.oxfordbus.co.uk and www.stagecoachbus.com). The City Sightseeing tour buses stop on Parks Road, very close the Museum (see www.citysightseeingoxford.com).

By rail: There are frequent rail services to Oxford from London and many other towns and cities. The railway station is off Frideswide Square, 15–20 minutes' walk from the Museum, or a short taxi ride.

Address:
Oxford University
Museum of Natural History,
Parks Road,
Oxford OX1 3PW

Telephone number:
+44 (0)1865 272950
Fax number:
+44 (0)1865 272970
Email: info@oum.ox.ac.uk
Website: www.oum.ox.ac.uk